Discover & Learn

Volcanoes & Earthquakes

This book is for pupils studying volcanoes and earthquakes in KS2 Geography (ages 7-11).

It's full of facts, diagrams and questions covering their physical and human aspects — perfect for exploring and understanding the whole topic.

Published by CGP
Consultant: Joanna Copley
Editors: Andy Cashmore, Mary Falkner, Kelsey Hammond, Sarah Pattison, Rebecca Russell
Reviewer: Alison Griffin
ISBN: 978 1 78294 973 2
With thanks to Alex Billings for the proofreading.
With thanks to Jan Greenway for the copyright research.
Printed by Elanders Ltd, Newcastle upon Tyne
Clipart from Corel®

Contents

Inside the Earth

What's at the centre of the Earth? That's a question we've being trying to answer for hundreds of years, with everything from explanations based on religious beliefs to scientific theories.

What do you think is at the centre of the Earth?

A vast, empty centre

Since ancient times, some people have believed that the Earth's centre is a hollow space. Different people had different thoughts about what might be in that empty place...

The Ancient Greeks believed that there were caverns underground which led to the underworld. This was a place where souls would go after death.

One religious Buddhist story tells of an ancient city inside the Earth called Shambhala. Only people who were pure of heart could find it and live there peacefully.

In the 17th century, some scientists thought the Earth was made up of a hollow shell. Some even believed that we lived on the inside of the shell and that the Sun was at the Earth's centre.

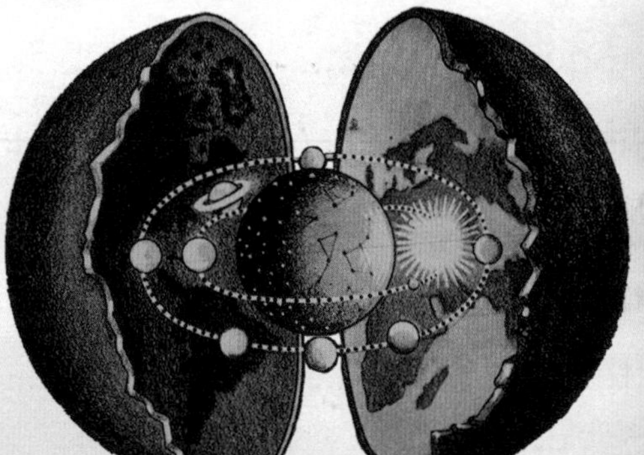

Full of fire

Early Christians believed that Hell was at the centre of the earth.

Hell was thought to be a very hot and fiery place where sinful people were sent to be punished after death.

The Earth is like a Cadbury Creme Egg®

Today, we know a lot more about what the inside of the Earth looks like.

If you could cut the Earth in half, you'd see that it looks a bit like a Cadbury Creme Egg — nice and solid on the outside with a gooey liquid bit inside.

The inside of the Earth is split up into different layers. Here they are:

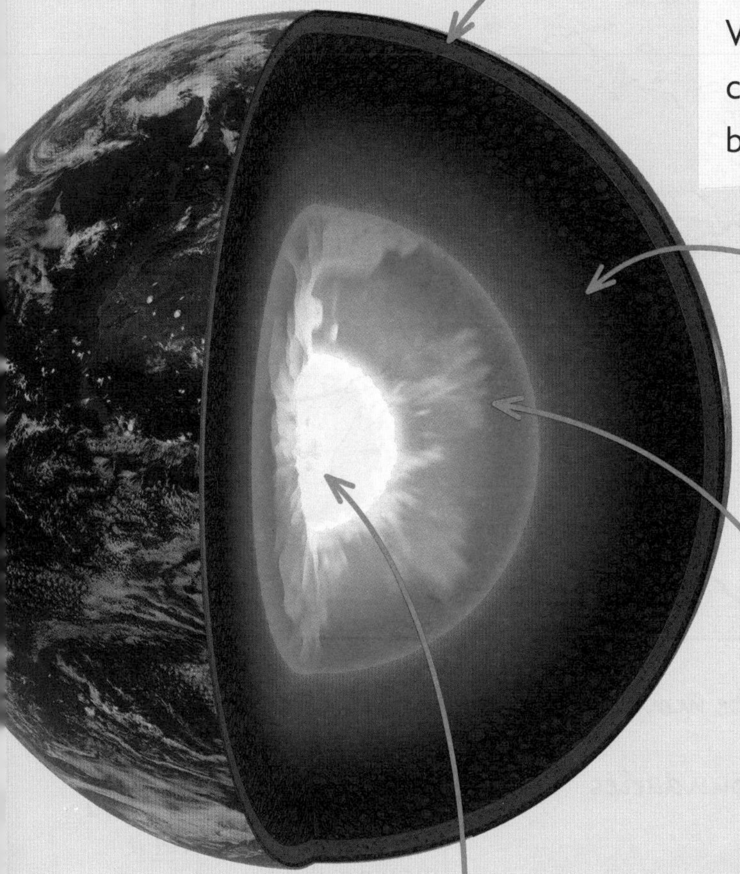

CRUST

The crust is the outer layer of the Earth. We live on its surface and parts of it are covered by oceans. It's really hard and solid, but is very thin compared to the other layers.

MANTLE

The mantle is a very thick layer of the Earth. It's made of hot molten rock called magma so it's like the gooey bit of a Cadbury Creme Egg, but really hot.

OUTER CORE

It gets even hotter as you get closer to the centre of the Earth. It's so hot that the outer core is a layer of liquid, which scientists think is made of the metals iron and nickel.

INNER CORE

The inner core is the centre of the Earth. It's the hottest part at about 6,000 °C, but there's so much pressure that it's solid, not liquid. It's a big, super-hot, solid ball of iron and nickel.

Look at the myths and theories on the previous page — do you think any of them were close to being correct?

No one's actually journeyed to the centre of the Earth...

Scientists have worked out that the Earth has layers by looking at other planets, doing lots of complicated maths problems and measuring the vibrations caused by earthquakes.

A Floating Crust

The Earth's surface seems nice and solid under our feet, but actually it's constantly moving. The thin crust that we live on is split up into pieces which 'float' on the mantle. The pieces are called tectonic plates. Waves of heat from the hot mantle make the plates move.

THE EARTH'S TECTONIC PLATES

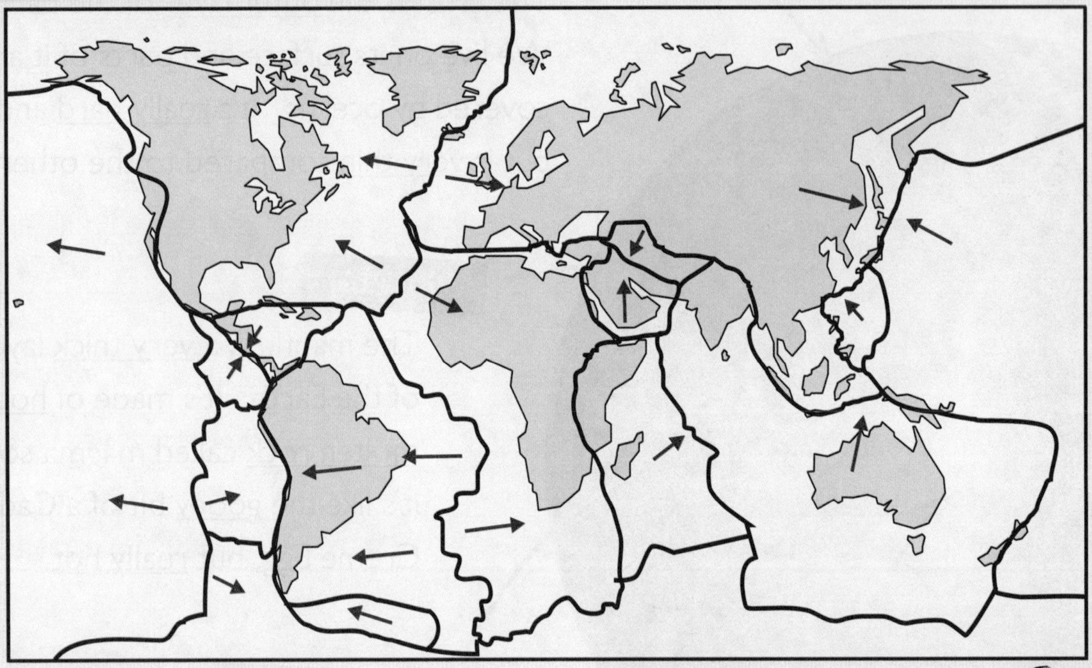

KEY

→ direction of plate movement

— tectonic plate boundaries

Can you find on the map the tectonic plate that you live on? Can you feel it moving right now?

Slow and steady...

Tectonic plates move at a very, very slow pace — just a few centimetres every year. In fact, the Atlantic plate underneath the USA moves away from Europe at around the same speed that your finger nails grow.

Over millions of years this adds up to thousands of kilometres. The world has changed shape a lot — land has pulled apart and come closer together.

Drifting apart

Today the world is made up of seven continents — large areas of land separated by oceans.

The Earth hasn't always looked like this. The continents were once all connected, but were slowly pulled apart by tectonic plates moving beneath the surface.

1. 225 MILLION YEARS AGO

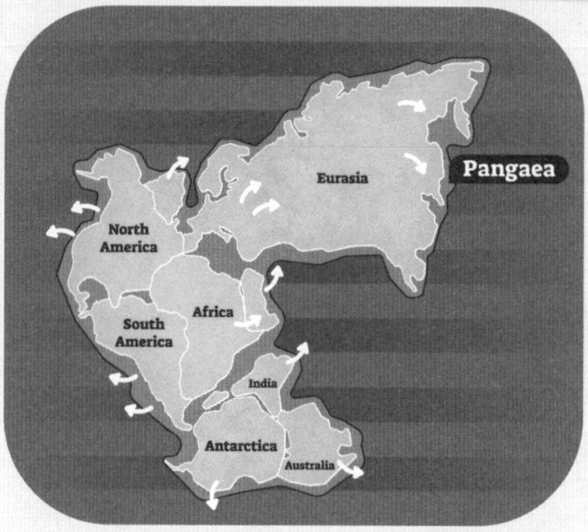

The world was once one giant piece of land. This supercontinent is known as 'Pangaea' ("pan-jee-a").

2. 200 MILLION YEARS AGO

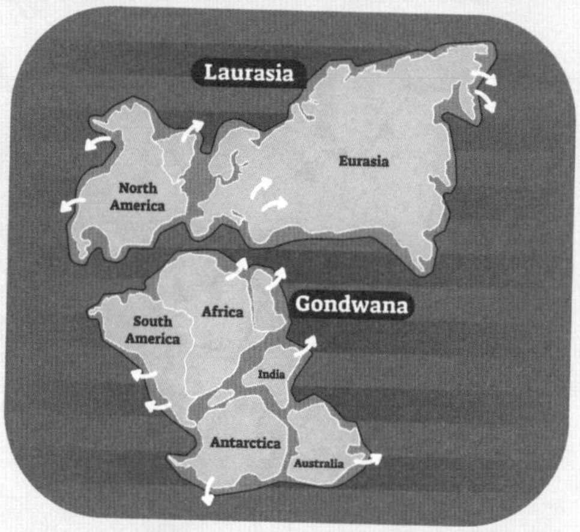

Over time, Pangaea broke apart into two areas — 'Laurasia' and 'Gondwana'.

3. TODAY

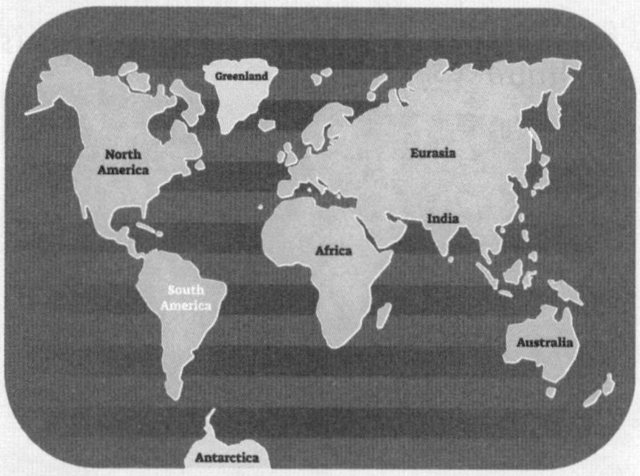

About 65 million years ago, our seven continents finally formed. This was around the same time that the dinosaurs went extinct.

Scientists predict that another supercontinent will form in the next 250 million years.

Tectonic plates may be slow, but they're powerful...

When plates bump together, they can cause destruction — turn the page to see how.

Clashes and Collisions

Earthquakes and volcanoes are usually found at plate boundaries (where two plates meet).

WHERE VOLCANOES AND EARTHQUAKES HAPPEN

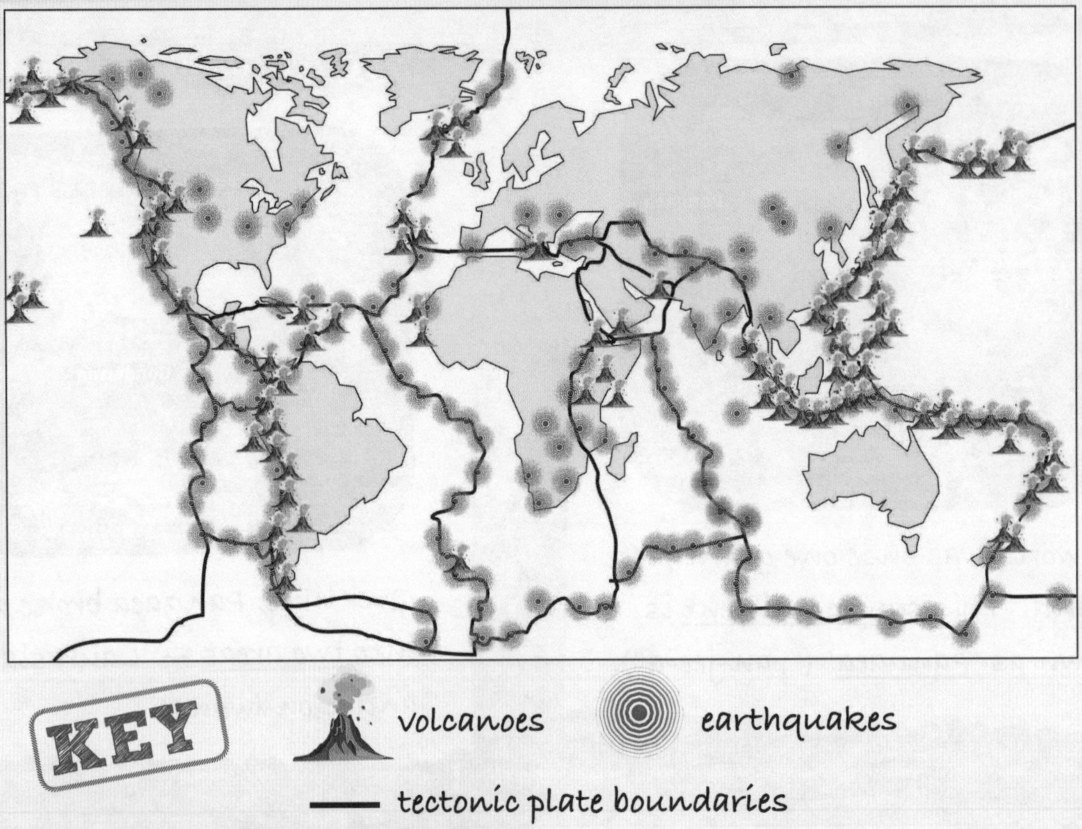

Plate boundaries aren't all the same. You can get conservative, destructive and constructive plate boundaries.

People in the UK don't feel many earthquakes. Why do you think this is?

Letting things slide

Conservative plate boundaries are where two plates slowly slide past each other in opposite directions.

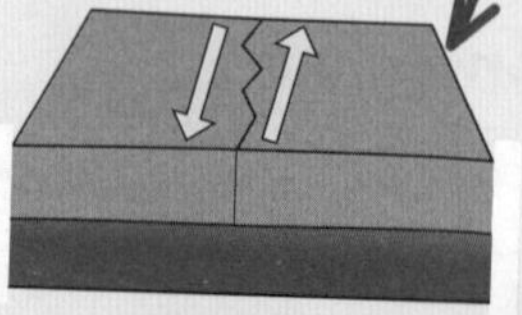

The edges of the plates are uneven, so when they slide past each other they can get a bit stuck. This causes pressure to build up. When the pressure is released suddenly it causes an earthquake.

Powers of destruction

<u>Destructive plate boundaries</u> are where two plates move <u>towards</u> each other.

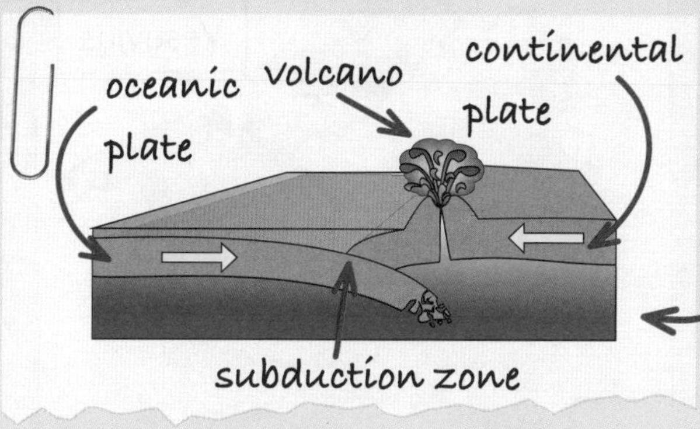

When an oceanic plate (a plate that's mostly under the sea) meets a continental plate (a plate that's mostly under land), the oceanic plate is forced <u>under</u> the continental one. The place where this happens is called a subduction zone.

The oceanic plate <u>melts</u> as it's forced downwards. This causes magma to <u>rise up</u> to the surface where it breaks through to form <u>volcanoes</u>. <u>Earthquakes</u> can also happen here as the two plates catch on each other.

Look at the map of the world on page 4. Which plate boundaries do you think might be destructive?

Let's get constructive

At <u>constructive plate boundaries</u>, plates <u>move apart</u> and the gap between them gets filled with <u>magma</u>. The magma <u>cools</u> when it reaches the surface and forms a new crust. Then it all happens again as the plates <u>keep moving</u>.

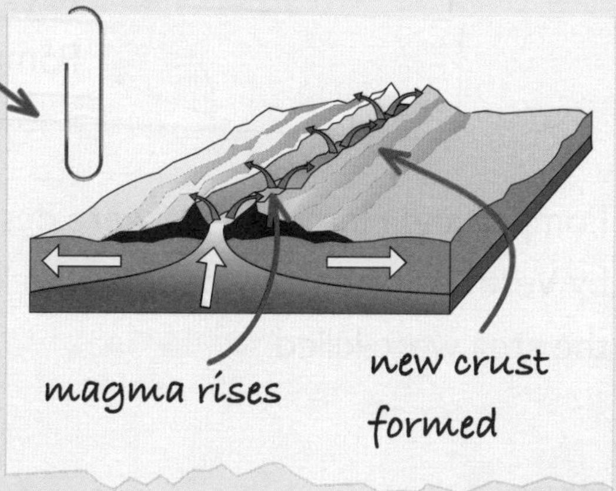

Sometimes the magma can rise up to form <u>volcanoes</u>. <u>Earthquakes</u> can happen at these plate boundaries too.

Mashing makes mountains...

It's not just volcanoes and earthquakes that are found at plate boundaries. You can find fold mountains too. These are made when two continental plates move towards each other — the edges where they collide are pushed upwards and this creates mountains.

Vesuvius

Vesuvius is a volcano on the west coast of Italy, near a city called Naples.

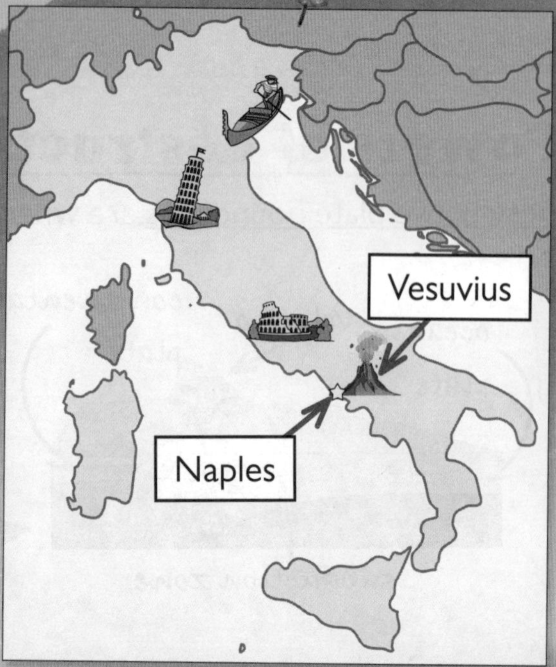

Fact Sheet: Mount Vesuvius

Height: 1281 metres
Location: Naples, Italy
Age: Approximately 17,000 years old
Last Eruption: 1944

Vesuvius's most famous eruption happened in 79 AD, nearly 2000 years ago. At this time, Romans lived nearby in the city of Pompeii and the holiday town of Herculaneum.

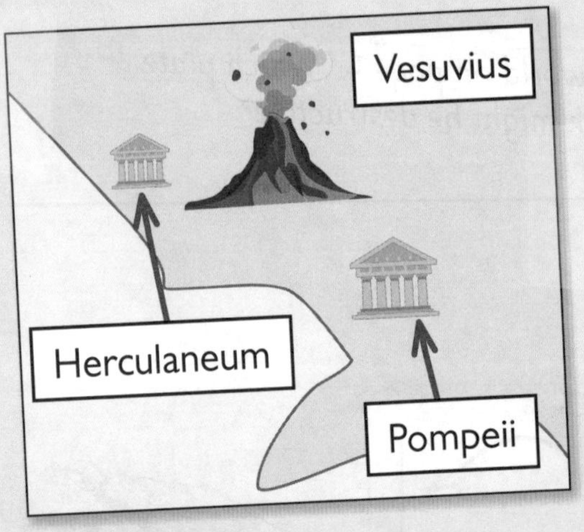

Pompeii and Herculaneum were destroyed by Vesuvius, and many people who lived in the area were killed.

Why live next to a volcano?

People lived near Vesuvius because the land was good for farming. Volcanic ash from previous eruptions made the soil fertile. This meant it was easy for farmers to grow fruit like grapes near Vesuvius.

Would you want to live next to a volcano?
~~NO~~ NO

Warning signs

In 62 AD, a powerful earthquake caused a large amount of damage to the area around Vesuvius. Pompeii and Herculaneum were both affected by this earthquake.

Small earthquakes also began to happen in 79 AD, four days before Vesuvius erupted. However, people living nearby didn't recognise this as a sign that the volcano was about to erupt. They thought the earthquakes were caused by gods.

My name is Claudia and I live in Pompeii. The ground has been shaking a lot recently, but we get earthquakes all the time in this part of Italy. It's nothing unusual and certainly nothing to be worried about. Everyone knows it's just the gods making the earth shake.

Beneath the surface

People at the time didn't know that the movement of tectonic plates caused earthquakes and volcanoes. They also didn't know that Vesuvius was above a subduction zone.

Below the ground, magma was building up, which would eventually cause the volcano to erupt.

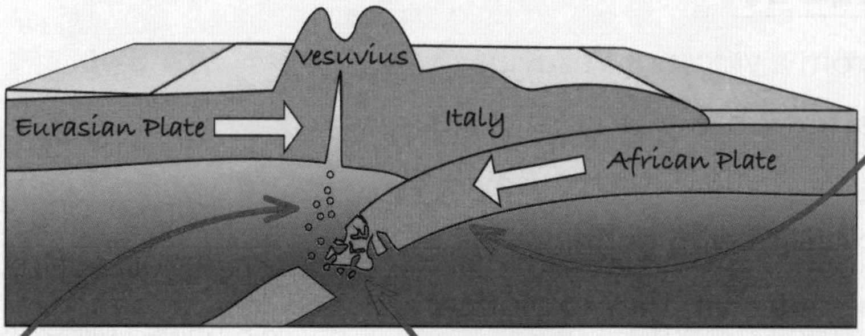

1 The African Plate is forced underneath the Eurasian Plate.

2 Part of the African Plate melts because of high temperatures in the mantle.

3 Magma builds under Vesuvius.

There's no smoke without fire...

The people living near Vesuvius were unaware that it was about to erupt. They didn't know how volcanoes worked, and were unprepared for the catastrophe to come...

Timeline of an Eruption

At 8am on the day of the eruption, a small cloud of ash appeared at the volcano's crater. This was the first sign above the Earth's surface that the volcano was active.

By 1pm the cloud was over 20 km high — that's higher than most aeroplanes fly. The cloud blocked out the sun and plunged the surrounding area into darkness.

A lack of lava flow

Unlike what you may expect from a volcano, Vesuvius didn't produce runny lava. (Lava is what magma is called when it reaches the Earth's surface). This is because the magma within Vesuvius was filled with bubbles. When the bubbles reached the outer air, they exploded.

Rocks, ash and gas are ejected from a volcano during an eruption. Vesuvius threw out rocks full of air holes called pumice.

Hot ash and pumice rained down on Pompeii in the afternoon. Buildings collapsed under the weight of the ash and stone. The heat caused fires to break out.

Voices from the past

We know so much about the eruption in 79 AD thanks to Pliny the Younger. He wrote letters to his friend after Vesuvius erupted to tell him what he had seen:

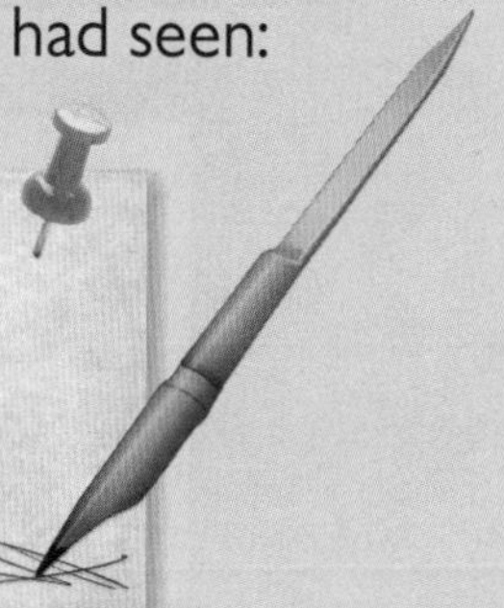

'I cannot give you a more exact description than by likening it to that of a pine tree, for it shot up to a great height in the form of a very tall trunk, which spread itself out at the top into a sort of branches'.

The elder sailor

Pliny the Younger also wrote about his uncle, Pliny the Elder. He sailed from a nearby town to Vesuvius to rescue his friend:

'He steered his course direct to the point of danger... He was now so close to the mountain that ashes, which grew thicker and hotter the nearer he approached, fell into the ships, together with pumice-stones, and black pieces of burning rock'.

Pliny the Elder found his friend, but they couldn't sail back because the wind was blowing in the wrong direction. To keep his friend calm, he served food and told him to take a bath. However, things started to get worse...

'The houses rocked from side to side with frequent and violent shocks as though shaken from their very foundations. In the open fields the pumice stones, though light indeed, fell in large showers'.

Pliny's demise

Rather than be buried under a collapsing house, Pliny the Elder and his friend tried to escape. They wore pillows on their heads to protect from the falling pumice stones.

Sadly, Pliny the Elder collapsed and died, possibly because of toxic fumes in the air. His body was discovered two days later, after the eruption had ended.

The Eruption Continues

As the afternoon went on, more fires broke out in Pompeii. The streets were buried in ash and pumice, trapping people inside their collapsing homes.

Herculaneum looked on

Herculaneum wasn't showered with volcanic stones like Pompeii, even though it was closer to Vesuvius. This was because the wind was blowing the ash and pumice stones away from Herculaneum.

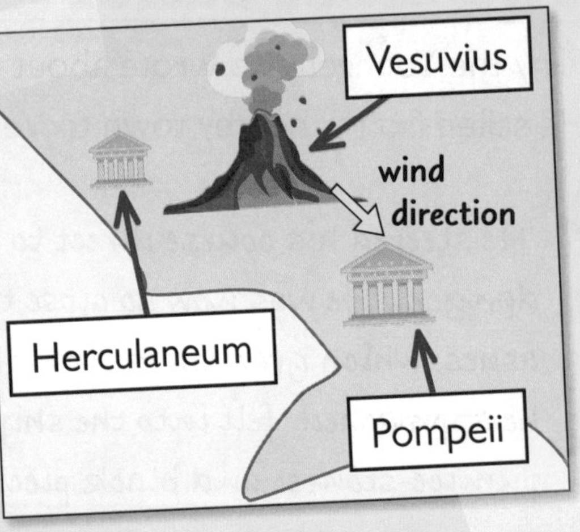

Why do you think some people may not have left Herculaneum?

The burning cloud

As Pompeii was smashed to pieces and set alight, the plume of smoke from Vesuvius was growing. The column of ash reached over 30 km high. Then, the worst happened...

At around midnight, the column of ash above Vesuvius collapsed under its own weight. A burning cloud of ash and gas rolled down the mountainside to Herculaneum. It killed everyone in the town. The cloud was so hot that it instantly turned everything it touched into ash or charcoal.

Pliny the Younger described the terror of the rolling ash clouds in one of his letters.

'The ashes now began to fall upon us, though not very thickly. I looked back; a dense dark cloud seemed to be following us, spreading itself over the country like a flood.'

The end of Pompeii

At six o'clock the following morning, the burning clouds swept over Pompeii. Anyone who was still alive was killed. The city was buried under 5 metres of ash and rubble.

Pompeii and Herculaneum were completely destroyed by Vesuvius.
No attempts were made to clear up the destruction after the eruption ended.

Frozen in time

Hundreds of years later, archeologists uncovered the ruins of Pompeii and Herculaneum. They found old wall paintings and the remains of buildings.

What do you think we can learn about the past from ruins like these?

The most fascinating discovery were the bodies of people living at the time of the eruption.

Their bodies were cast in hardened ash, preserving them as they were in 79 AD.

A city and a town vanished in a day...

There were many stages to the destruction of Pompeii and Herculaneum. The eruption of Vesuvius shows how volcanoes can cause devastating damage in lots of different ways.

Types of Volcano

Not every volcano erupts in the same way that Vesuvius did.

Volcanoes can have explosive eruptions that shoot rocks, ash and gas high into the air...

...or effusive eruptions in which liquid lava flows down the side of the volcano.

What type of eruption do you think Vesuvius had?

The type of eruption depends on what's inside the volcano...

Taking a closer look at volcanoes (but not too close!)

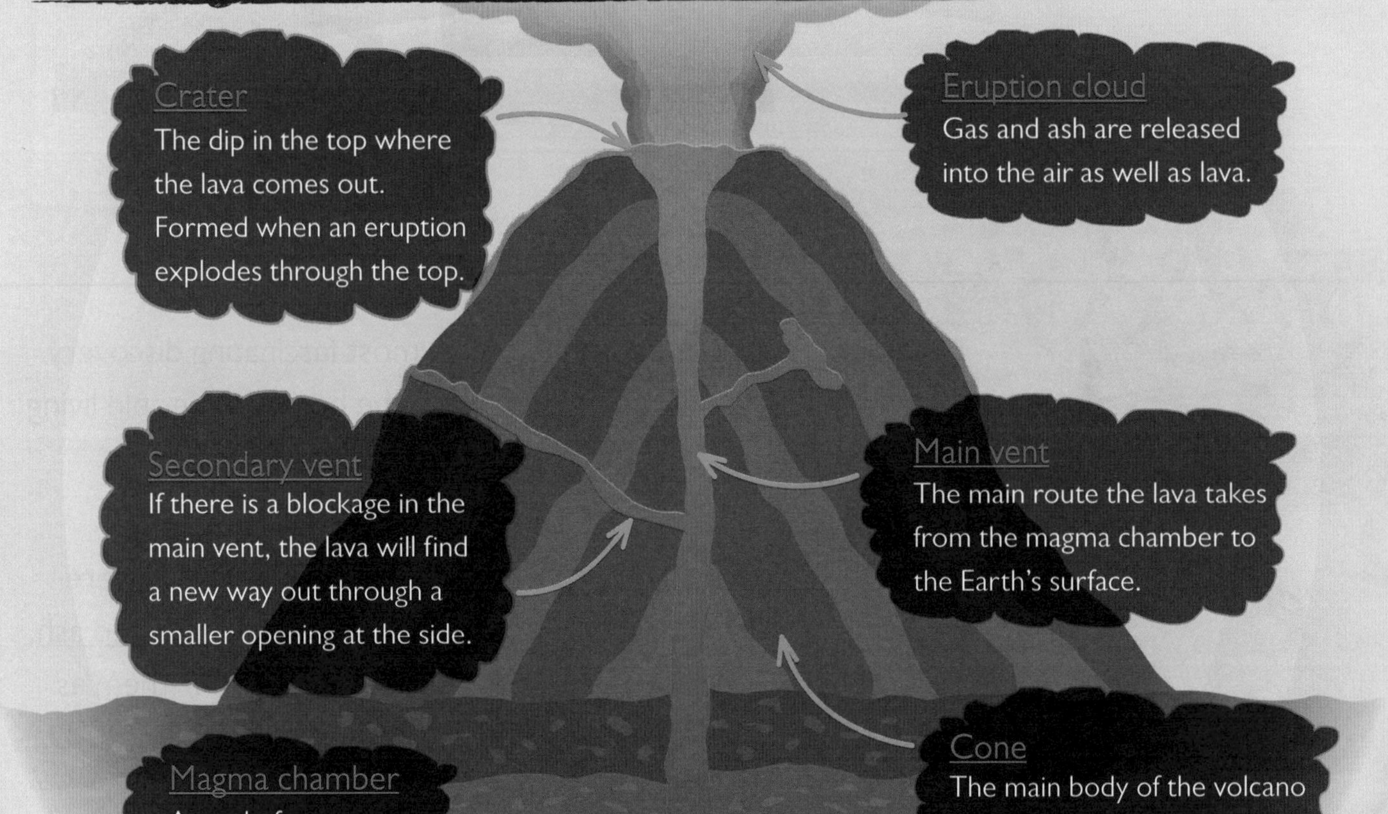

Effusive eruptions are caused by hot, runny magma that flows from the volcano.
Explosive eruptions are caused by thick, bubbly magma that blows apart at the surface.

Many shapes and sizes

The type of eruption affects what a volcano looks like. An explosive eruption drops rocks and ash around the cone and any lava doesn't flow very far — this gives the volcano steep sides. Runny lava from an effusive eruption travels a long way and hardens to form a gentle slope.

Here are three types of volcano which are formed in different ways:

STRATOVOLCANO

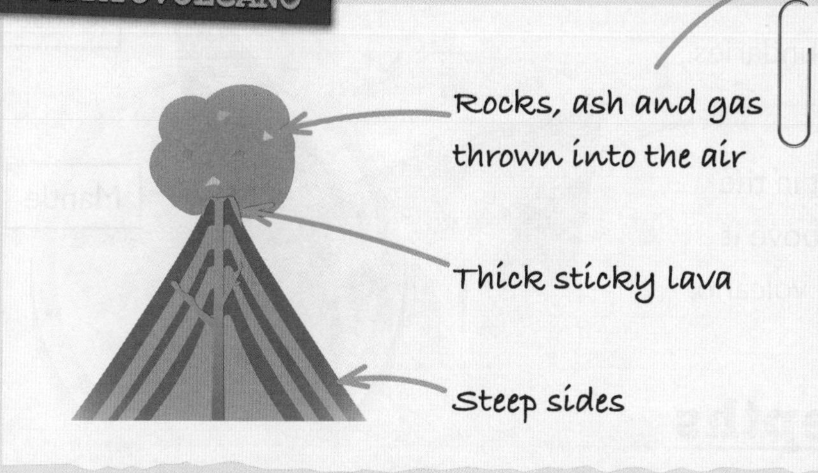

SHIELD VOLCANO

CINDER CONE

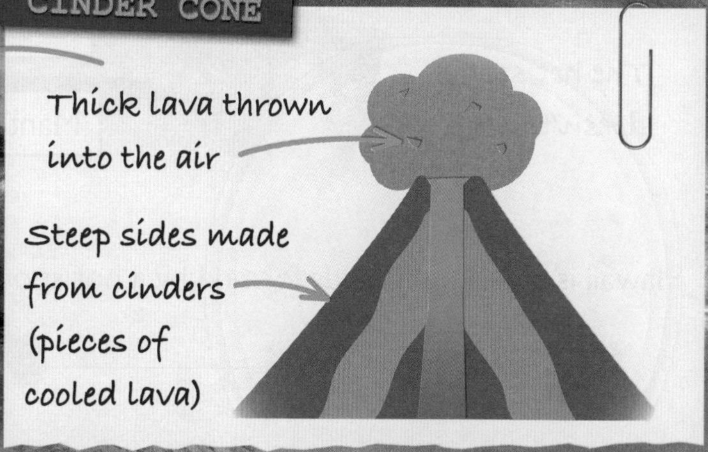

A volcano that's out of this world...

We have some pretty big volcanoes on Earth, but the biggest one in our solar system is actually on Mars. It's a shield volcano called Olympus Mons — it's more than twice the height of Mount Everest and covers a larger area than the whole of the UK. That's big!

Volcanoes in the Deep

You might not be able to see it but there is plenty of volcanic activity happening in our oceans. Volcanic eruptions can happen above the water, and beneath it too.

Concentrated heat

Volcanoes don't just form at plate boundaries. They can also form at hot spots.

A hot spot is an area of extreme heat in the mantle (see p.7). It melts the crust above it and magma bursts through to form a volcano.

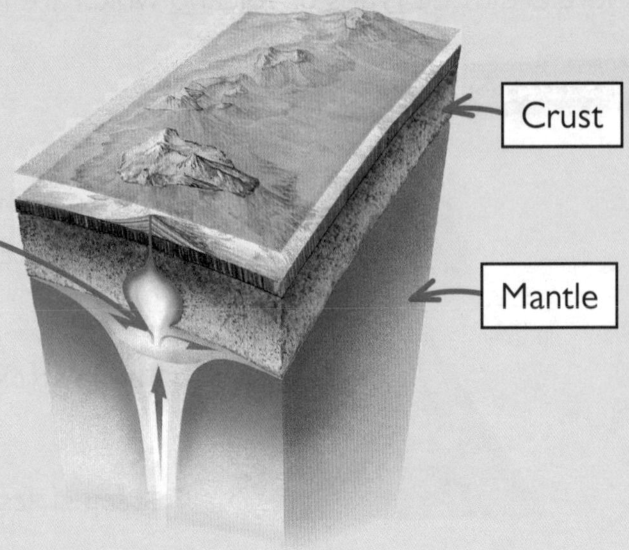

Rising from the depths

Hot spots can also create chains of new islands. This happens when the tectonic plate moves like a conveyor belt over a hot spot:

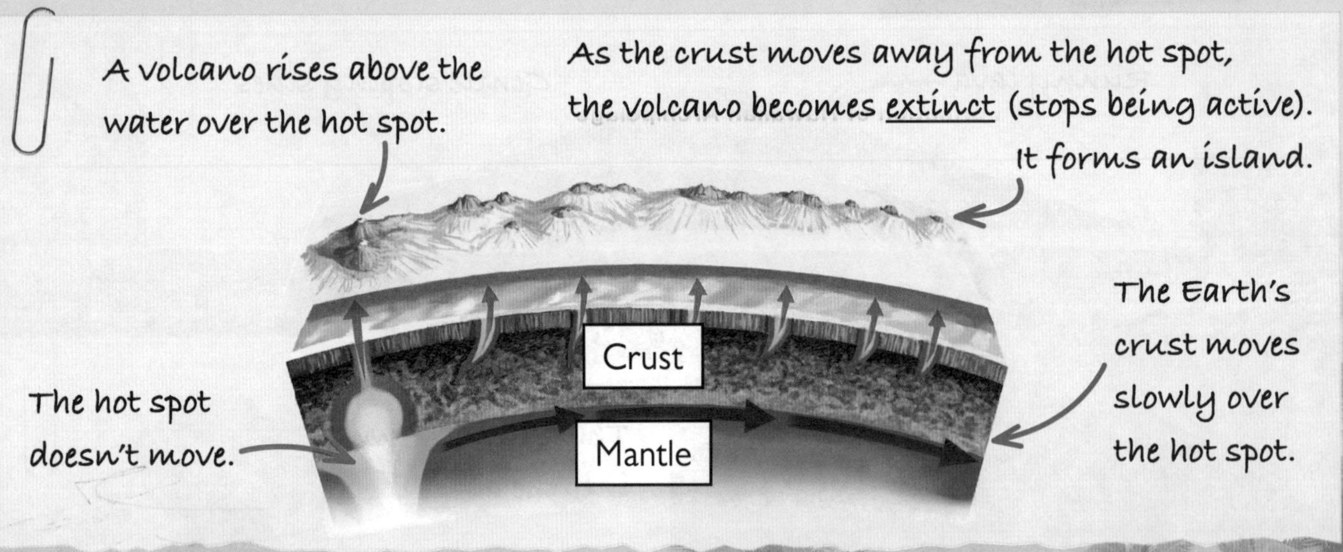

Hawaii is a chain of islands formed by a hot spot. The chain is still growing today.

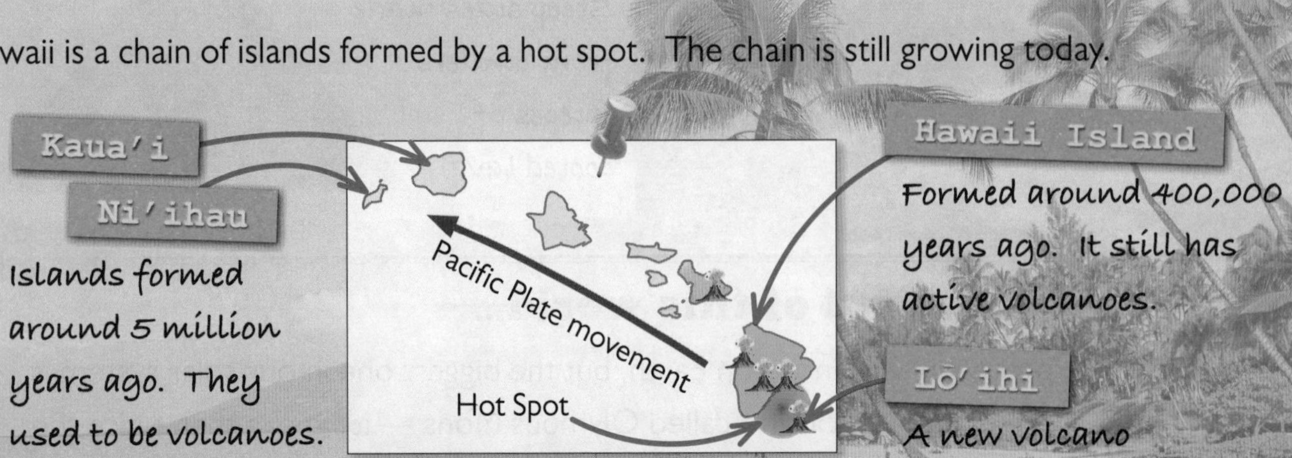

Avinash

Smoke in the water

Volcanic eruptions at plate boundaries under the sea cause lava and water to mix together to form superheated sea water. The eruptions also form fissures (large cracks) in the rocks.

The hot sea water dissolves minerals and gets pushed up out of the fissure. When the hot water hits cold sea water, the minerals form crystals and fall around the fissure. The minerals build up and eventually create large towers called black smokers.

The beginning of life

Scientists used to believe that all life on Earth needed sunlight to survive. However, creatures such as giant tube worms were found near black smokers where there was no sunlight.

These creatures feed on special bacteria that survive on the chemicals produced by black smokers. The bacteria are the start of the food chain around the smokers (like plants are the start of our food chain).

Scientists now think that life may have begun around black smokers.

Many secrets remain about volcanoes under the sea...

It's only recently that scientists have been able to study underwater volcanoes, partly because they are thousands of metres below sea level. There's still a lot to be learnt.

San Francisco

Fact Sheet: San Francisco

Country: West coast of California, USA.

Population today: About 880,000

Size: About 120 km² (47 square miles)

Number of tourists visiting every year: Around 25 million

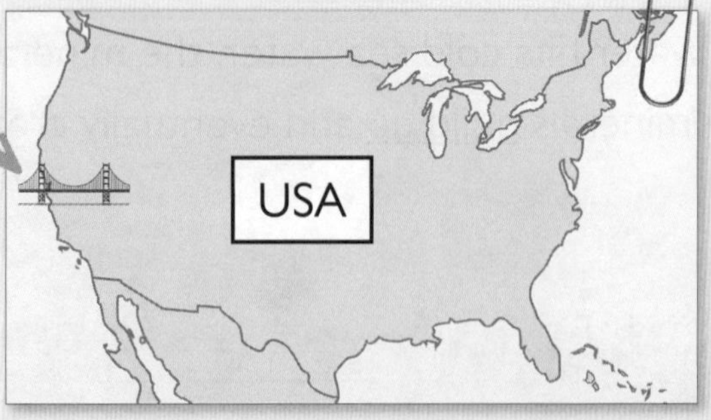

San Francisco is a city in the USA. It is popular with tourists from around the world.

Many people come to San Francisco to see the Golden Gate Bridge and the old prison on Alcatraz Island.

City of earthquakes

San Francisco is also well known for its earthquakes. Earthquakes happen here every single day.

Most of the earthquakes that happen are so weak that people don't notice them.

But a number of large earthquakes have hit San Francisco in the past. Some of them caused lots of damage.

The San Andreas Fault

The area around San Francisco has so many earthquakes because it sits on the San Andreas Fault. This is a section of a conservative plate boundary (see p.6) that's over 800 miles long.

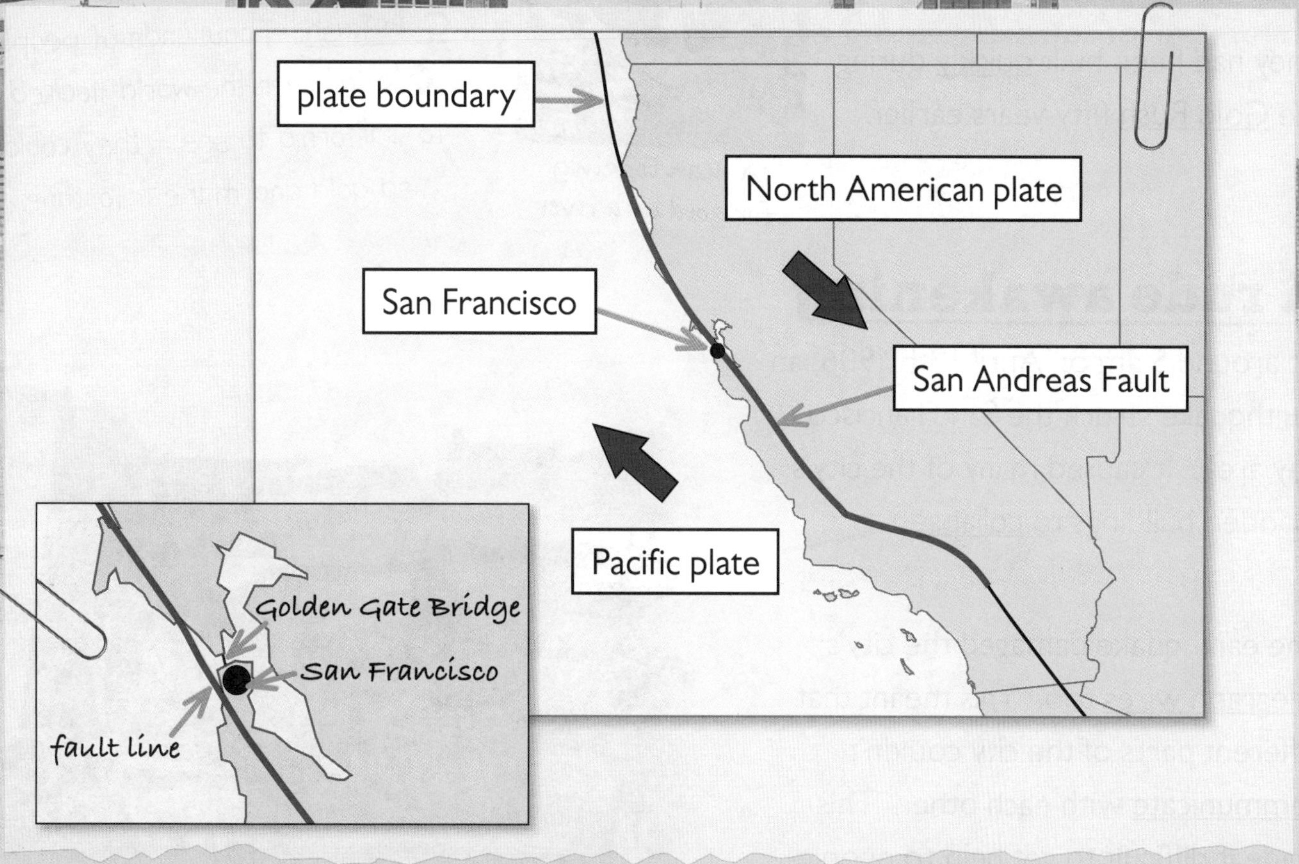

The North American plate and the Pacific plate slide past each other in opposite directions. This creates pressure which builds up, and is eventually released in the form of an earthquake.

Would you want to live in San Francisco?
Why do you think so many people choose to live there?

Life on the boundary...

In 1906, San Francisco was hit by the most powerful earthquake the city had ever experienced. But San Francisco wasn't built to resist an earthquake that big. Turn over the page to read about this earthquake and what happened to the city...

The 1906 Earthquake

In 1906, San Francisco was a booming city. It was home to around 400,000 people, making it the largest city on the West Coast of the USA.

Most of the buildings in the city were made from wood.

They had been built quickly during the Gold Rush fifty years earlier.

A man looking for gold in a river

When gold was discovered in California in 1848, it started the Gold Rush. Thousands of people from all over the world flocked to California to see if they could find gold and make a fortune.

A rude awakening

At around 5 am on April 18th 1906, an earthquake struck the San Francisco Bay area. It caused many of the city's wooden buildings to collapse.

The earthquake damaged the city's telegraph wires too. This meant that different parts of the city couldn't communicate with each other. This made it difficult to get help to people.

Fire (and ham and eggs)

The earthquake caused great damage, including breaking gas pipes all over San Francisco.

The broken gas pipes and wooden buildings led to many fires. Before long, there were over thirty small fires across the city.

One of the largest fires started when somebody was cooking their breakfast — so it was called the 'Ham and Eggs Fire'.

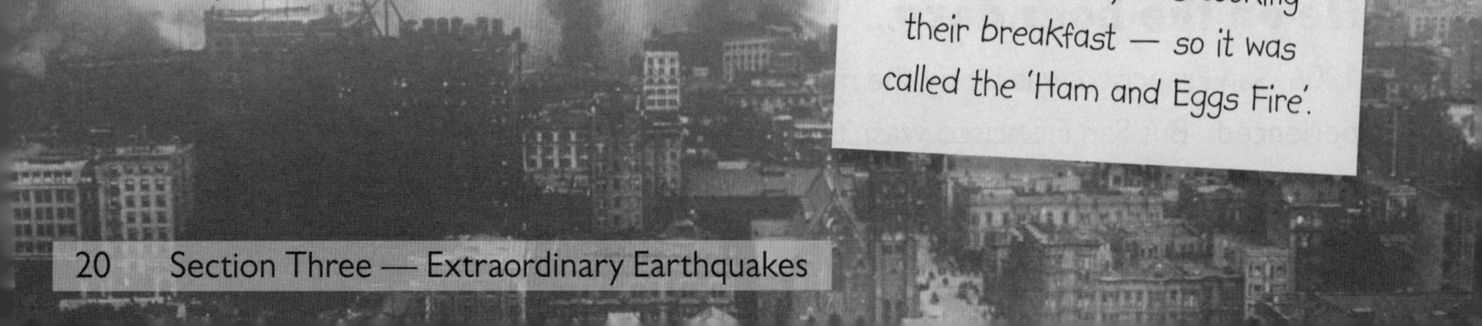

Firefighters without water

San Francisco had a very well-trained fire department with horse-drawn fire engines. However, they came up against the fire fight of their lives...

We are firefighters from the San Francisco Fire Department. We fought the flames all morning, but in the early afternoon we ran out of water. The earthquake had broken the water pipes! We searched everywhere trying to find more water. It wasn't long until the fires grew out of control...

Without water to stop the fires, the flames grew.

The small fires that had started in the morning joined up into one huge fire.

The firefighters were helpless.

A city in flames

The massive fire created firestorms. Firestorms happen when a fire gets so large that it begins to suck in huge amounts of air. This creates a strong wind around the fire. Firestorms are so dangerous because the wind can carry the fires great distances very quickly.

The firestorms spread easily across San Francisco because of the broken gas pipes. They set alight the destroyed wooden buildings and kept the fire going.

The fires showed no signs of letting up...

The earthquake created enough damage and chaos to allow fire to take over San Francisco. The city's leaders had to react to save lives and buildings — but also to restore order.

After the Earthquake

20 PAGES TODAY
ST. LOUIS POST-DISPATCH
FOURTH EXTRA
SAN FRANCISCO BURNING UP!
Earthquake Topples Down Hundreds of Buildings, Killing or Injuring 1500 Persons; Tidal Wave Sweeps Water Front.

In total, the fire burned through San Francisco for three days before it was put out.

During this time, there was a lot of panic and crime in the city that needed to be controlled.

General's orders

General Frederick Funston was in charge of some soldiers at a nearby fort when the earthquake happened. He brought his soldiers from the fort to help the city.

Funston got his soldiers to blow up rows of houses with dynamite. He thought the gaps would stop the fire spreading. But it didn't work — the fallen buildings caught fire.

Looting and shooting

People began to loot (steal things) from shops and homes that had been abandoned during the earthquake. To prevent this, Funston sent soldiers to patrol the streets.

The Mayor of San Francisco told the police and soldiers to shoot looters. Due to the confusion and chaos in the city, this led to some innocent people being shot...

I am a soldier who patrolled the streets after the earthquake. Most of us worked hard to keep the peace, but I heard stories about innocent people being killed. One soldier shot a man who he thought was stealing a chicken, but it actually belonged to the man.

Camping in the city

Many people were left homeless because of the earthquake.
Some of these people left on the ferry to go to nearby towns and cities.

Others stayed in San Francisco and lived in tents put up in parks and on beaches.

It took more than two years to get everyone back into ordinary housing.

Would you have preferred to stay in a tent in your home town or leave for a new town?

Fact Sheet: San Francisco 1906 Earthquake

Deaths: More than 3,000 people
Homeless: 250,000 people
Buildings destroyed: 28,000 (80% of city)
Cost of damage: About $500 million

In 1906, $500 million would be worth about the same as $14 billion today.

Rising from the ashes

Things would have been very bleak for those who had lost their homes and loved ones.

A lot of support and money was given by people all around the world to help San Francisco recover. In just three years, the city had been rebuilt.

A chance to build better...

Because San Francisco had been built in a hurry during the Gold Rush, it hadn't been planned very well. One of the few good outcomes of the earthquake was that it gave the government the opportunity to rebuild the city so that it had more modern buildings.

Earthquake Information

When scientists investigated the 1906 San Francisco earthquake, one of the most important things they found was that it had been caused by moving tectonic plates.

What makes the Earth quake?

Earthquakes happen where tectonic plates get stuck as they slide past each other. Pressure builds as the plates try to move until they suddenly jerk past each other. The pressure is released in waves of energy. This causes the ground to shake.

The place on the ground that is directly above where the earthquake starts is called the epicentre.

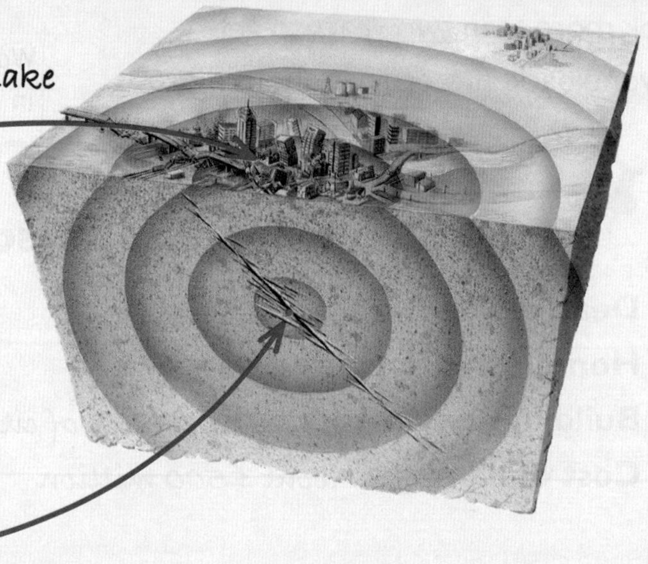

The further away you are from the epicentre, the less you feel an earthquake.

The exact place underground where an earthquake happens is called the focus.

Sometimes there are smaller earthquakes before the main one, called foreshocks. There will often be smaller earthquakes after the first one, called aftershocks.

What's shaking?

A machine called a seismometer can record the Earth's shaking. Scientists can use this tool to tell where an earthquake happened.

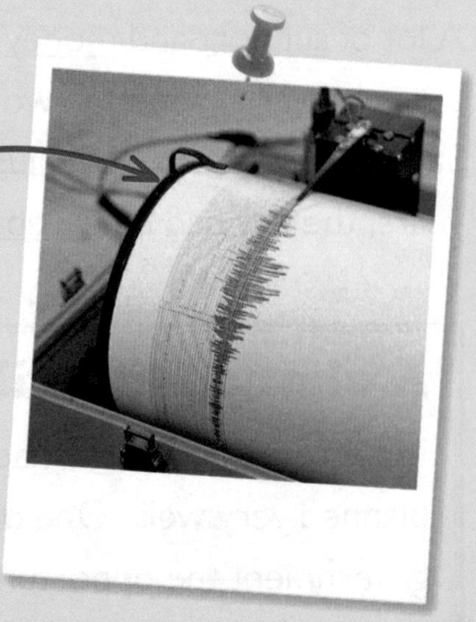

The strength of the shaking is measured using the Richter scale. On the Richter scale, each level of earthquake is ten times stronger than the one before. So an earthquake measuring 4 is ten times more powerful than one measuring 3.

Big earthquakes, big problems

Here are some examples of big earthquakes and what they measured on the Richter scale...

SAN FRANCISCO, 1906

Richter scale reading: 7.9

ITALY, 1908

Most destructive European earthquake

Richter scale reading: 7.5

CHILE, 1960

Most powerful recorded earthquake

Richter scale reading: 9.5

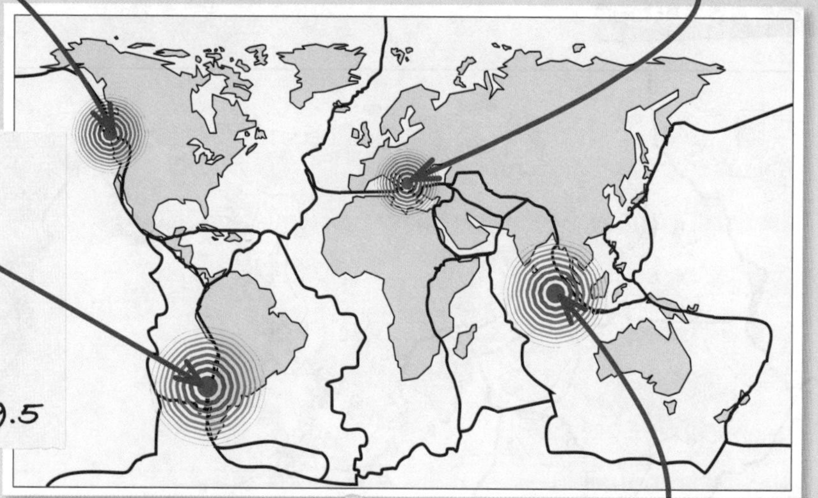

Some earthquakes that happen at sea or near the coast cause a tsunami. A tsunami is a very large wave that floods the land.

INDONESIA, 2004

225,000 dead, mostly from a tsunami

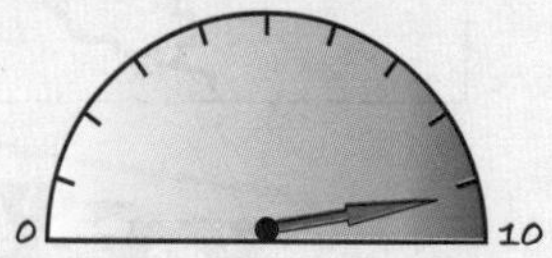

Richter scale reading: 9.1

Where, but not when

We can get an idea of where powerful earthquakes may happen by looking at plate boundaries and the movement of tectonic plates.

When lots of small earthquakes happen in the same place, it can be a signal that a big earthquake is coming soon. But we can't predict exactly when earthquakes will happen.

Earthquakes are happening all the time

Over a million earthquakes happen every year all over the world, but many are so small that we just don't notice them. Even the UK has about 200 earthquakes every year.

Troubled Earth

Most of the world's volcanoes are found at the edges of tectonic plates. This is also where earthquakes are most likely to happen.

The area around the Pacific Ocean contains 75% of the Earth's volcanoes and has about 90% of the world's earthquakes. Because of that, this area is called the "Ring of Fire".

RING OF FIRE

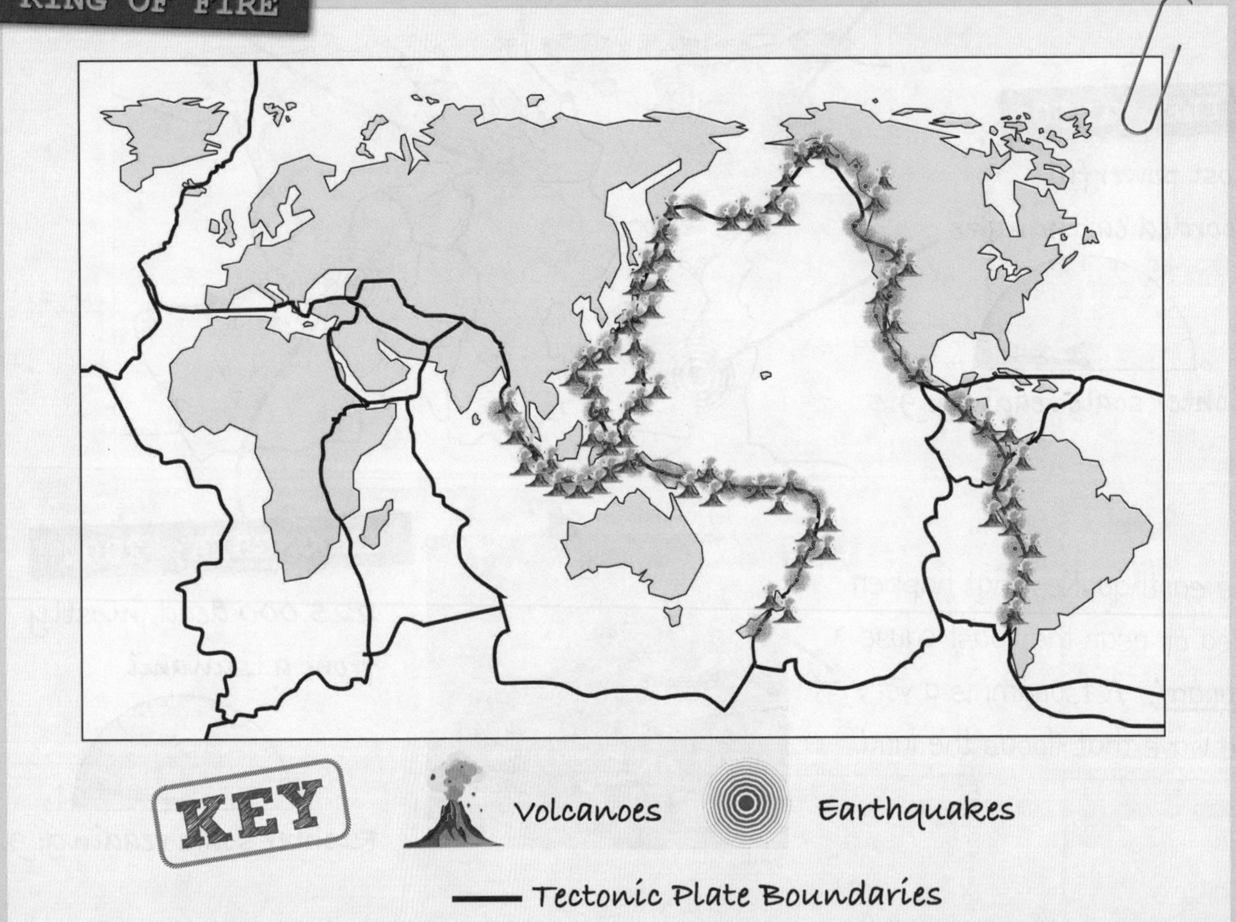

Lots of countries that are in the Ring of Fire take steps to prepare for earthquakes and volcanic eruptions.

But many countries in this area are poor, so they don't have much money to spend on preparing for disasters. These places are often hit hardest by the effects of volcanic eruptions and earthquakes.

Unruly neighbour

In spite of the risks, many people choose to live in areas that are near the edge of tectonic plates. There can be benefits to living in these places:

- Money from tourism — many people come to visit volcanoes.
- Fertile soil — ash from volcanoes makes the land good for farming.
- Mining — rocks formed from lava can contain valuable minerals such as copper and gold.
- Stunning views — imagine waking up to that everyday.
- A source of energy — see below.

Would any of these reasons be good enough to persuade you to live somewhere in the Ring of Fire?

The power of the planet

Lots of heat is stored in the rocks below the Earth's surface. This heat can be used to generate electricity. This type of energy is called geothermal energy.

Most power stations that use geothermal energy are built in countries that have lots of volcanoes, like Iceland. In places near volcanoes, the ground is very hot not far below the surface — so it's easier to get at the heat than it would be in other places.

The big benefit of geothermal energy is that it's renewable — that means it will never run out.

Dangerous but useful...

Lots of people live near volcanoes, or in places that get lots of earthquakes. It has its advantages, but it's risky too. So we need to find ways to help keep these people safe.

Keeping Safe — Prediction

There are three Ps that we can use to help keep people safe from a volcanic eruption or an earthquake. The first of these is prediction. Knowing when a disaster is about to strike and reacting to warnings can make the difference between a few deaths and thousands.

Mount St Helens, 1980

Mount St Helens is a volcano in the USA, North America. A massive eruption happened at Mount St Helens on 18th May 1980.

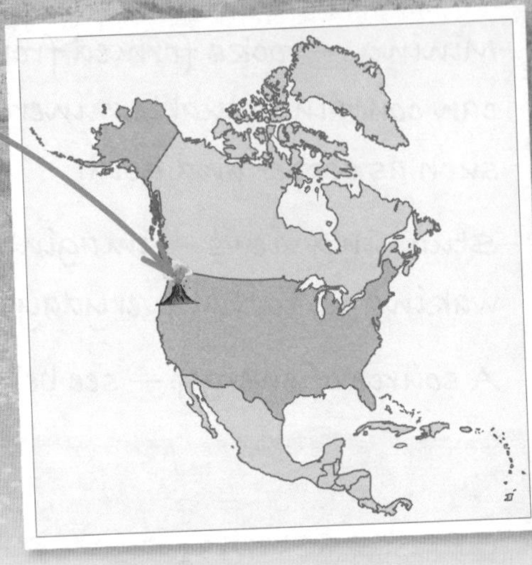

Two months before the eruption, scientists recorded small earthquakes near the volcano. These got stronger and more frequent. The volcano also let out steam and ash.

When the volcano did erupt, it was one of the largest eruptions ever recorded. Despite the fact that lots of people live fairly near to the volcano, only 57 people were killed.

PREDICTION SAVES LIVES

Scientists had been monitoring Mount St Helens for a long time and were able to tell well in advance that it was at risk of erupting. When they predicted that it was likely to erupt soon, the government acted on this by advising people to leave the area.

The USA is a rich country, so they were able to spend money on studying the volcano closely and taking action in case it erupted. This probably saved many lives.

Nevado del Ruiz, 1985

Nevado del Ruiz is a volcano in Colombia, South America. It erupted on 13th November 1985. The eruption was 100 times less powerful than the eruption at Mount St Helens.

The year before the volcano erupted, it began to release steam and smoke. In the months leading up to the eruption, lots of small earthquakes were recorded near the volcano too.

When Nevado del Ruiz erupted, it created huge rivers of mud and rocks that flowed down the volcano and swept towards the local towns. Even though the eruption was much less powerful than the one at Mount St Helens, it killed about 21,000 people.

PREDICTION WITHOUT ACTION

When Nevado del Ruiz had been showing signs of activity for a while, scientists began to study it. They warned that the volcano was at risk of erupting.

Although it's possible to predict that a volcano is going to erupt, it's very hard to predict exactly when it will happen.

Colombia was quite a poor country. The government could not afford to spend a lot of money getting people out of the area without being sure that the volcano was going to erupt soon. They did try to evacuate people when it actually began to erupt, but by then it was too late.

Acting on predictions saves lives...

Scientists monitor volcanoes and plate boundaries for signs of upcoming eruptions or earthquakes. That way, action can be taken to protect people nearby.

Keeping Safe — Prevention

The second of the three Ps is prevention. It's impossible to prevent volcanic eruptions and earthquakes from happening. But there are ways to prevent them affecting as many people.

Get out right now!

The best way to prevent a volcano harming people is to evacuate the area if it might erupt.

Volcano Evacuation Plan

If you live near a volcano:

- Make sure you know where the nearest shelter is and how to get to it.
- Listen to local warning systems for updates.

If you are told to evacuate:

- Leave as soon as possible.
- Avoid using roads or paths that could be at risk from lava or landslides when the volcano erupts.
- If ash is falling, wear goggles and long clothing to protect yourself.

A successful evacuation

The 1991 eruption of Mount Pinatubo in the Philippines was one of the largest eruptions in the last 100 years. Thousands of people live near Mount Pinatubo.

American scientists studying Mount Pinatubo knew it was getting ready to erupt. They gave warnings about when the eruption was likely to happen and how much damage it would do. This gave people time to evacuate to a safe distance, which saved many lives.

Building for a safer future

Buildings can be constructed to <u>resist earthquakes</u>.
One way of doing this is to build them on top of beams rather than straight on the ground. The beams <u>move</u> with the earthquake, but the building above stays still.

Doing this is <u>expensive</u>. In areas where there isn't the money to build things like this, there are simpler things you can do:

Earthquake Resistant Houses

- Walls can be made stronger by building them around a frame made of bamboo rods, which are strong but cheap.
- Packing straw into the middle of plaster walls means that the walls can resist more shaking before they collapse.
- Roofs made from thin sheets of metal resist earthquakes better than concrete roofs (and are less likely to hurt people if they do collapse).

Taking a hit

In 2015, Nepal was hit by a massive earthquake.
Around 9,000 people died and <u>four million</u> were made homeless.

Many houses in Nepal weren't built to resist earthquakes.

But the small number of simple, <u>earthquake resistant</u> homes survived.

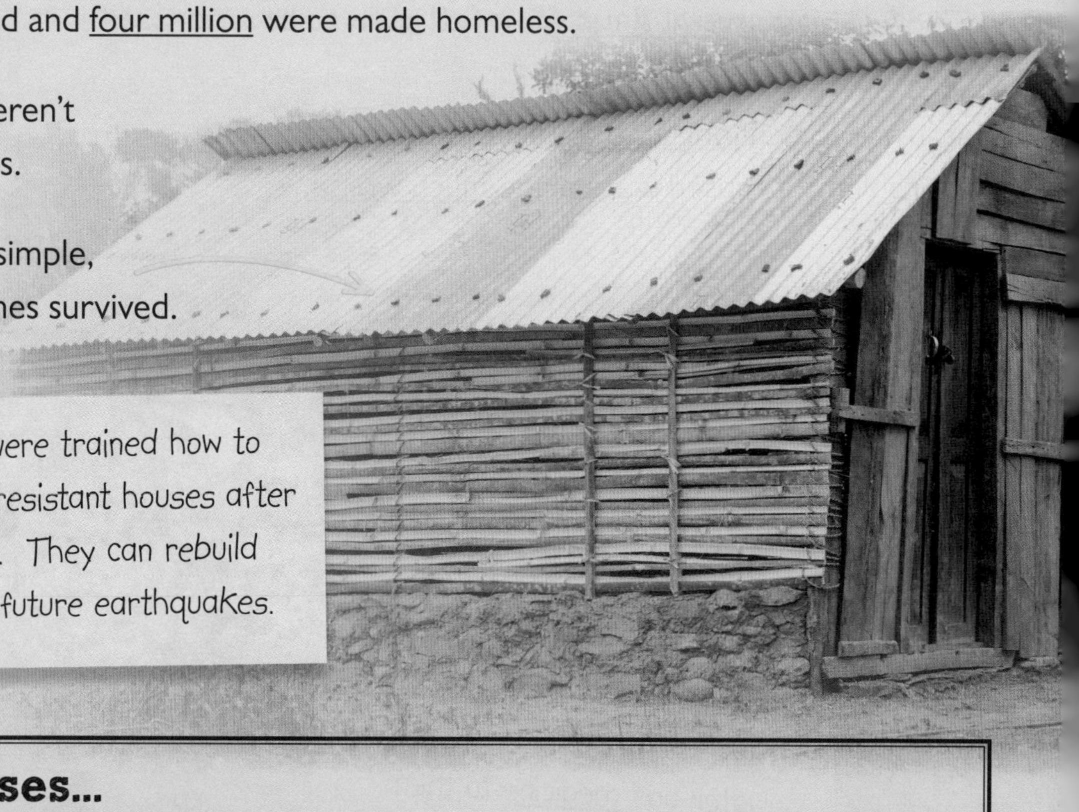

Local builders were trained how to build earthquake resistant houses after the 2015 quake. They can rebuild homes to resist future earthquakes.

As safe as houses...

It can be fairly cheap to build earthquake resistant houses — and they can save lives.

Keeping Safe – Preparation

The final P is preparation. Countries can prepare for a disaster by making sure that hospitals, police and the government know what to do if a disaster hits. It's also important to have emergency supplies ready. A plan of action can help save lives.

Haiti, 2010

Haiti is a small country in the Caribbean Sea. On 12th January 2010, a big earthquake hit Haiti.

Haiti wasn't prepared for the earthquake.

2010, Haiti

Strength:

Richter scale reading: 7

- People hadn't been told what to do to keep safe during an earthquake.
- After the earthquake hit, there was a lot of confusion about who was in charge of dealing with the problems that it caused.
- It took several days for a full plan to be organised.

Because it took a long time to react to the earthquake, the problems it caused were made much worse.

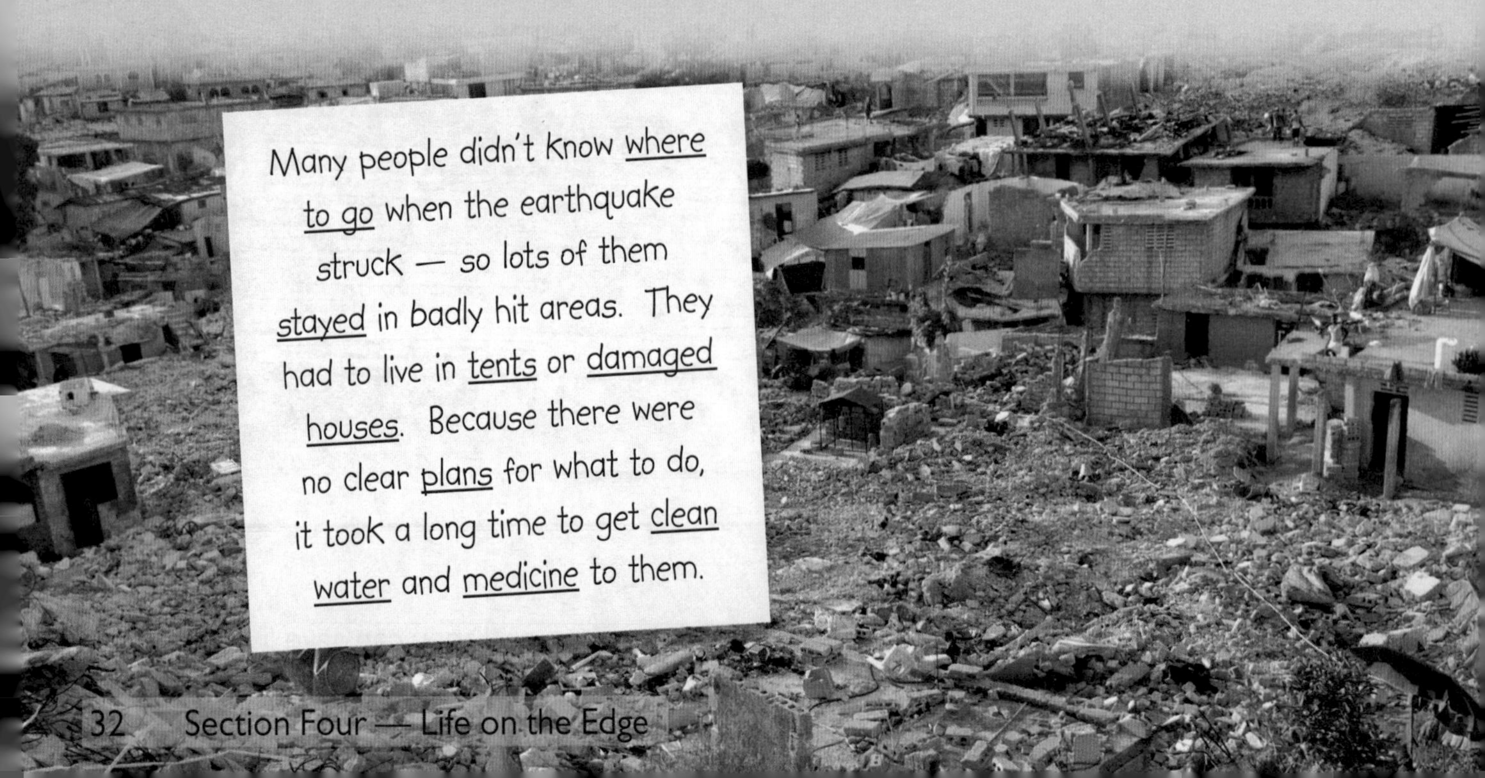

Many people didn't know where to go when the earthquake struck — so lots of them stayed in badly hit areas. They had to live in tents or damaged houses. Because there were no clear plans for what to do, it took a long time to get clean water and medicine to them.

Japan, 2011

Japan is a country in the Pacific Ocean. On 11th March 2011, a huge earthquake hit Japan.

This caused a tsunami (giant wave), which swept 6 miles inland and killed a lot of people.

Japan was well-prepared for the earthquake.

2011, Japan

Strength:

Richter scale reading: 9

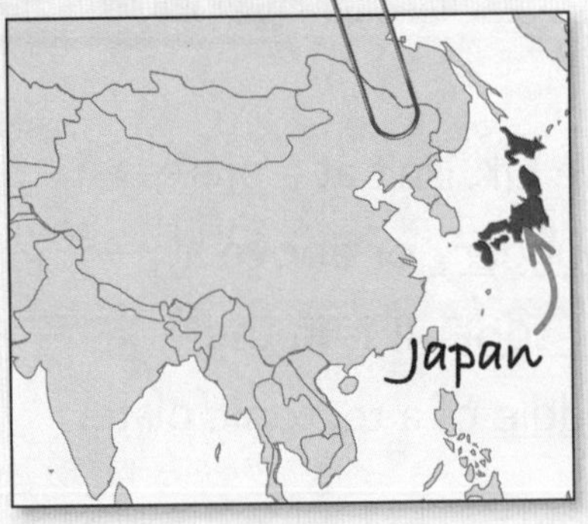

- Regular earthquake drills meant that people had practised how to keep safe.
- A warning system sent an alert to mobile phones just before the earthquake.
- Four minutes after the earthquake, the Japanese Prime Minister put an earthquake plan into action.
- Within an hour, police and rescue workers were on their way to damaged areas.

Not much damage was caused by the earthquake. But people weren't as prepared for the tsunami. This was more deadly than the quake.

There were warnings that a tsunami was coming, but it turned out to be bigger than expected. This was partly why it caused so much damage.

Why do you think Japan was so well prepared for an earthquake, but Haiti wasn't?

Ready for action!

The earthquake that struck Japan was one of the most powerful ever recorded. But because they were prepared, they were ready to swing into action with a sensible plan.

All Calm in the UK?

The UK isn't at a plate boundary or above a hot spot. It is in the middle of a tectonic plate.

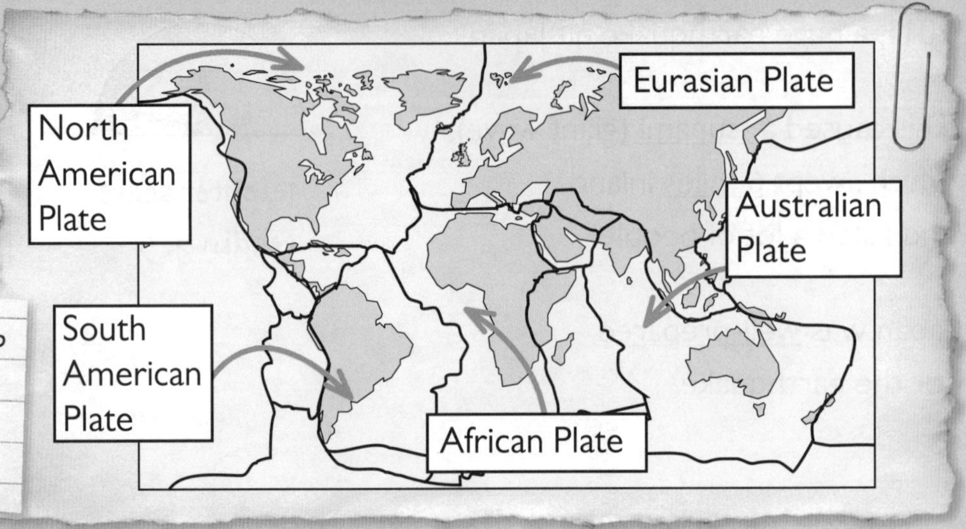

Which plate is the UK on? Can you point to the nearest plate boundary to the UK on the map?

A shaky past

Many earthquakes happen every year in the UK, but they're usually weak. Only a few are felt each year. In the past, there have been a few bigger ones...

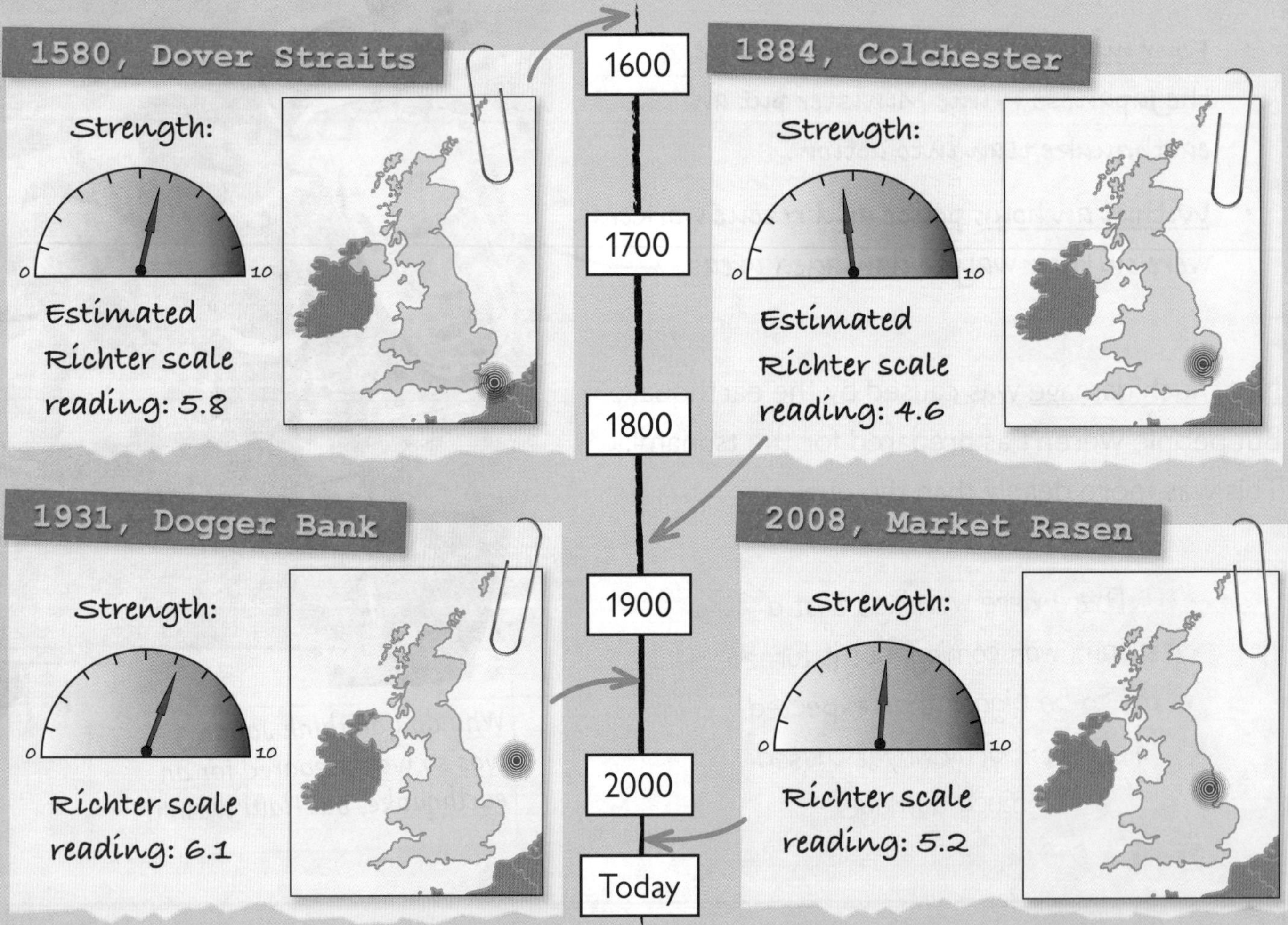

The UK isn't on a plate boundary but it still gets earthquakes because of cracks in the plate it sits on. Cracks are formed when a plate is bumped or when it slides past other plates. As the plate moves, there are small movements at the cracks that can cause earthquakes.

Many years ago there were volcanoes in the UK. All the volcanoes in the UK are now extinct (never going to erupt again) but you can still see evidence of them today...

Castle Rock

The volcano underneath Castle Rock in Edinburgh was last active 340 million years ago. Edinburgh Castle was built on the volcano in the 12th Century AD, many years after it became extinct. It's now a popular tourist destination.

Castle Rock is a volcanic plug. It was formed by magma hardening inside the volcano vent.

Giant's Causeway

These rock columns in Northern Ireland are famous around the world. They were created by volcanic activity 50-60 million years ago.

Giant's Causeway was formed when lava was forced up to the Earth's surface. This created a layer of lava on the shore which cooled to form thousands of columns.

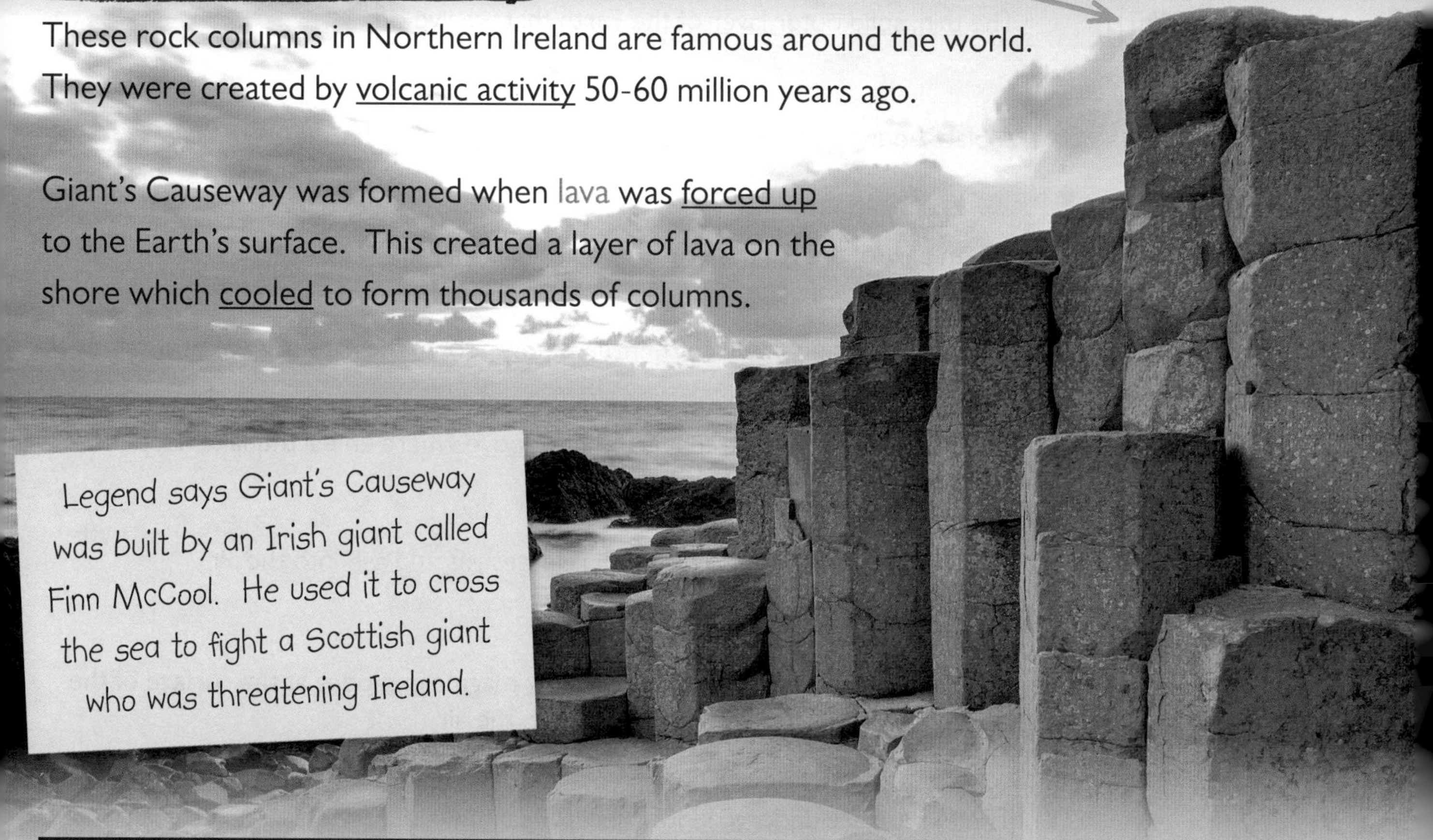

Legend says Giant's Causeway was built by an Irish giant called Finn McCool. He used it to cross the sea to fight a Scottish giant who was threatening Ireland.

No volcanoes around here these days...

That's because tectonic plates have moved the UK away from a plate boundary. When it used to be closer to a plate boundary, the UK had volcanoes and more earthquakes.

Glossary

aftershock	A small earthquake that happens after the main earthquake.
cone (volcano)	The main body of a volcano.
conservative plate boundary	A plate boundary where the two plates slide past each other.
constructive plate boundary	A plate boundary where the two plates are moving away from each other.
continent	A large mass of land and the islands closest to it. The Earth has seven continents.
continental plate	A tectonic plate that is mostly under land.
crater (volcano)	The hole in the top of a volcano where lava comes out.
crust (of Earth)	The thin, solid outer layer of the Earth that we live on.
destructive plate boundary	A plate boundary where the plates move towards each other.
earthquake	When part of the Earth's crust wobbles and shakes.
effusive eruption	A type of eruption in which runny lava flows down the side of a volcano.
epicentre	The place on the ground that is directly above where an earthquake happens.
eruption cloud (volcano)	A cloud that forms when a volcano releases gas and ash into the air.
explosive eruption	A type of eruption in which thick, bubbly magma explodes at the surface of the volcano, throwing rocks, ash and gas into the air.
focus	The exact place underground where an earthquake happens.
fold mountain	An area of mountains formed by continental plates pushing together.

foreshock	A small earthquake that happens before the main earthquake.
geothermal energy	Energy from heat stored in rocks below the Earth's surface.
inner core (of Earth)	A super-hot, solid ball of iron and nickel at the centre of Earth.
lava	Magma that comes to the Earth's surface, for example from volcanoes.
magma	Hot liquid rock underneath the Earth's surface.
magma chamber	A pool of magma in the Earth.
main vent (volcano)	The main route the lava takes from the magma chamber to the Earth's surface.
mantle (of Earth)	The thick, gooey layer of molten rock underneath the Earth's crust.
minerals	Small, solid substances that make up rocks.
oceanic plate	A tectonic plate that is mostly under the sea.
outer core (of Earth)	A hot, liquid layer of iron and nickel surrounding the Earth's inner core.
Richter scale	A scale used to measure the strength of earthquakes.
secondary vent (volcano)	When there is a blockage in the main vent of a volcano, the lava flows through this smaller opening at the side of the volcano.
subduction zone	An area where two tectonic plates meet and one plate is forced underneath another plate.
tectonic plates	Pieces of the Earth's crust that float on the mantle.
volcano	An opening in the Earth's crust which can let hot magma and ash escape to the surface as a volcanic eruption.

Acknowledgements

Some paragraphs in this book include characters and dialogue which has been invented for dramatic purposes – any similarity to a person, living or deceased, in these areas is merely coincidence.

Graphics used through this book: (push pin) © iStock.com/blackred. (lined paper) © iStock.com/subjug. (torn paper) © iStock.com/Tolga TEZCAN

Section One — The Restless Earth
p2 (hollow earth) Mary Evans Picture Library. p2 (hell) Mary Evans Picture Library. p3 (earth's core) JOHAN SWANEPOEL / SCIENCE PHOTO LIBRARY. p7 (Himalayas) © iStock.com/AndrzejStajer.

Section Two — Violent Volcanoes
p8 (Pompeii) © Harry Green/Look and Learn. p9 (Roman woman) © French School/Look and Learn. p10 (eruption at Pompeii) The Eruption of Vesuvius at Pompeii in 79 AD (colour litho), Niccolini, Antonio (1772-1850) (after) / Private Collection / Archives Charmet / Bridgeman Images. p11 (Pliny's death) © R Marti/Look and Learn. p11 (Pliny the Elder) SHEILA TERRY / SCIENCE PHOTO LIBRARY. p12 (pyroclast) STEPHEN & DONNA O'MEARA / SCIENCE PHOTO LIBRARY. p12 (Pompeii on fire) DAVID HARDY/SCIENCE PHOTO LIBRARY/Getty Images. p14 (volcano diagram) © iStock.com/jeremkin. p16 (Hawaii hot spot) GARY HINCKS / SCIENCE PHOTO LIBRARY. p16 (Hawaii under surface) SPENCER SUTTON / SCIENCE PHOTO LIBRARY. p17 (black smoker) JOSE ANTONIO PENAS / SCIENCE PHOTO LIBRARY.

Section Three — Extraordinary Earthquakes
p20 (collapsed wood buildings) Mary Evans Picture Library. p20 (San Francisco 1906 fire) UC REGENTS, NATL. INFORMATION SERVICE FOR EARTHQUAKE ENGINEERING / SCIENCE PHOTO LIBRARY. p21 (firefighters) Mary Evans / Everett Collection. p21 (street fire) UC REGENTS, NATL. INFORMATION SERVICE FOR EARTHQUAKE ENGINEERING / SCIENCE PHOTO LIBRARY. p22 (soldier in San Francisco) © Sergio Toppi/Look and Learn. p22 (newspaper) © John Frost Newspapers/Mary Evans Picture Library. p22 (General Funston) Mary Evans / Everett Collection. p22 (smoke) LIBRARY OF CONGRESS / SCIENCE PHOTO LIBRARY. p23 (clearing debris) © American Photographer/Look and Learn. p23 (tents) Mary Evans / Everett Collection. p24 (earthquake diagram) GARY HINCKS / SCIENCE PHOTO LIBRARY. p24 (seismometer) ZEPHYR / SCIENCE PHOTO LIBRARY. p25 (tsunami) CHRIS BUTLER / SCIENCE PHOTO LIBRARY. p25 (1908 Italy) US NAVY / SCIENCE PHOTO LIBRARY.

Section Four — Life on the Edge
p27 (geothermal power station) PHIL DEGGINGER / SCIENCE PHOTO LIBRARY. p28 (Mount St Helens) © iStock.com/GarysFRP. p30 (Mount Pinatubo) David Hodges / Alamy Stock Photo. p33 (rescue worker) SPUTNIK / SCIENCE PHOTO LIBRARY.

Inside Cover
(old blank paper) © iStock.com/tomograf.

GVR21